C000227152

BRITISH MOTORCYCLES

TRIUMPH

BRITISH MOTORCYCLES
TRIUMPH

First published in the UK in 2013

© Demand Media Limited 2014

www.demand-media.co.uk

Printed and bound in Europe

ISBN 978-1-909217-61-4

Contents

Introduction

Beginning life in 1887 as a bicycle manufacturing company, The Triumph Cycle Company went on to become today's Triumph Motorcycles Limited. Since motorcycle production commenced in 1902, the Triumph factory has produced thousands of classics designs and is regarded as being producers of some of the world's finest motorcycles, from the original Bonneville in 1959 to today's models.

The name Triumph is a globally renowned and respected one in the world of motorcycles, with the company showcasing British engineering, design and production at its very best. Triumph have long been associated with sport, the first success at which can be dated back to 1908 when Jack Marshall won the Isle of Man race, setting the fastest lap. It was, however, the First World War that really threw Triumph into the forefront of motorcycle production; they supplied over 30,000 machines to the allied forces.

With the original factory destroyed during the Second World War, their new site built at Meriden in the British midlands became synonymous with Triumph's motorcycle production. The factory was the heartbeat of the company from 1940 to 1983. With the purchase of the company in 1983 by John Bloor, the company has undoubtedly seen it's ups and downs, but today, now with production based at Hinckley in Leicestershire, the Triumph factory produces 16 different models to satisfy enthusiasts on every continent.

With regard to this book, the intention here is to open up an image archive for others to see just some of the Triumph pictures that have been taken over the years. Nothing clever or complicated has been attempted here – though the book is split into time period sections, which is as far as we've gone in 'organising' things. We've even left the images in their raw untouched form, complete with period markings. We could have gone for a chronological order; we could have written plenty more words, but what we are trying to capture is something of the appeal of physically looking in the myriad boxes of pictures we have here. One never quite knows exactly what is where and what will be found. That is the thinking behind the way the publication has been put together.

The Triumph name is one of the most enduringly popular names in motorcycling. It is an evocative title, one that conjures up all sorts of powerful imagery while the word itself – triumph – literally means to

win. What a great name with which to christen your product.

Triumph the motorcycle maker has for the most part in its 100-plus years been a success story; a triumph, in fact. The idea of this tome is to celebrate, through a selection of images, that success story.

Hopefully, this Triumph edition will be the precursor to variations and there are many more pictures of this magnificent motorcycle manufacturer to be showcased in a similar way, should the demand be there for it of course. It's all about trying to enable what's been, largely, hidden in boxes for years, to be seen. We very much hope that you enjoy what has been selected here.

Getting Started: The Early Years – 1886-1913

Triumph as a brand began in 1886 when young London-based German entrepreneur Siegfried Bettmann reckoned he needed a new name for his fledgling bicycle-building business, rather than tagging the cycles with his own name. Bettmann had come to Britain in 1884 and initially worked for Kelly's, a company which published directories. In 1885 young Siegfried – born in Nuremburg, Bavaria but fluent in English and French – decided to branch out on his own and set up an import/export business, having worked in a number of jobs establishing contacts.

The go-ahead Bettmann initially exported Coventry-built motorcycles bearing the Bettmann name before switching to the Triumph moniker in 1886. Triumph was born. In 1887, another ambitious young German named Mauritz Schulte was recruited to the infant company and then in 1888 Bettmann, Schulte and Triumph moved to Britain's centre of cycling, the city of Coventry.

Premises were found in Much Park and rented from local politician, Albert Thompson. Indeed, not only was Thompson the landlord but he was significantly impressed enough by the two young Bavarians to invest, in partnership with local financier Alfred Freelander, to the tune of £2000 in the company. Bettmann and Schulte now

Left: *RW Ayton,
1905 3hp*

had powerful local allies and as Bettmann managed to raise another £500 from family connections for investment and Schulte only £150, it gave Bettmann a 70 per cent shareholding advantage over Schulte.

The Coventry based firm now went from strength to strength. Schulte, particularly, had an interest in motorcycles and was keen to branch out into powered two-wheeled manufacture. Meanwhile, Dunlop had been impressed by the company and persuaded Harvey du Cros to invest a whopping £45,000 in the Triumph concern. No longer was Triumph a struggling minnow – the company was becoming a big player in the two-wheeled world and the natural progression was into motorcycles.

In 1902, Schulte fitted a Belgian-built Minerva engine into a Triumph cycle and the first Triumph motorcycle was created. Belgian company Minerva was at the time regarded as among the best units available and though JA Prestwich (JAP) and Fafnir proprietary engines were used, by 1905 Triumph was making its own engine in-house. It was a remarkable progression – in just three years Triumph had progressed from bolting an engine to a cycle frame, to a producer of complete motorcycles.

The thing was that as well as becoming established quickly, Triumph built a good product. The first Triumph engine was a 363cc side-valve, for which

Above: *Mr McFarlane, of McFarlane Ironfounders, Chapel Lane, Wigan, at the controls of his 1913 Triumph*

Right: *Running in water, 20 minutes without a stop*

Centre:
JH Watson, November 1910

3hp was claimed. There was nothing flash or complicated about the engine – it was just well engineered and carefully put together and soon the Triumph reputation was growing.

By 1907, a 453cc engine was being made – that was upped to 476cc in 1908, then 499cc in 1910. Meanwhile,

though, a second design of engine was also introduced to run alongside the initial motor.

At the first Isle of Man TT in 1907, Triumph's Jack Marshall and Frank Hulbert finished second and third in the single cylinder class – a result that Marshall improved the next

Above: *Aluminium single barrel*

Right: *JR Haswell, TT practice, June 1912*

year, winning the class on what was possibly the world's first purpose-built racer. Other endurance runs, including Reverend Basil H Davies' (aka Ixion)

200 mile epic in 1906 and then the efforts of Ivan Hart-Davies and Albert Catt, all helped to ensure Triumph was well and truly on the map.

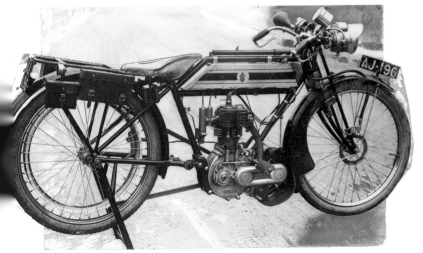

BRITISH MOTORCYCLES : **TRIUMPH**

11

Above: *Mr and Mrs CC Cooke of North Mimms, Hatfield – 3hp models*

Centre: *Baby Triumph, 1914*

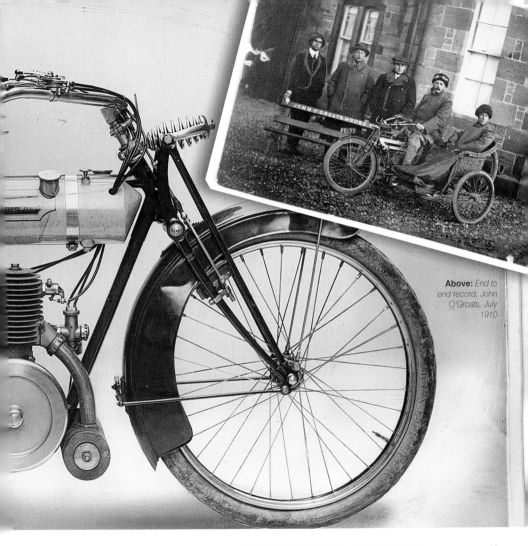

Above: *End to end record, John O'Groats, July 1910*

BRITISH MOTORCYCLES : **TRIUMPH**

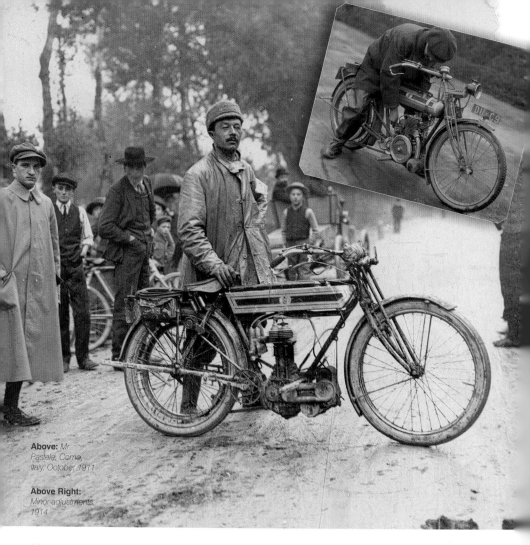

Above: *Mr
Pastela, Como,
Italy; October 1911*

Above Right:
*Minor adjustments,
1914*

The Great War: A Time of Conflict – 1914-1918

Far Right: *The Indian Army Corps stop in a French market square on their way to the front, October 1916*

Far Top: *A variety of parts.*

When Great Britain found itself at war in August 1914, the British government was quick to realise that this was to be a war where technology was to play an important part. Aircraft, tanks and indeed motorcycles were to be tested for the first time in real conflict.

The British military wanted a simple to operate, reliable machine – and so the men in power turned to Triumph. Surely, it must have been a somewhat strange situation for the men behind the Triumph concern. Of course, Bettmann and Schulte had long resided in England and indeed at the outbreak of war, Bettmann was ensconced as mayor of Coventry. Whatever his personal feelings may have been, when Captain

Claude Holbrook, for the war office, requested 100 motorcycles to be packed and despatched to France, Bettmann obliged. Indeed, Holbrook was to become a personal friend of Bettmann and was invited to join the board of Triumph following the cessation of hostilities.

The model despatched to France initially was a modified Model A, but it was succeeded by the immortal Model H, which was to become a bastion of the military with around 30,000 supplied over four years. It was in design nothing special, nothing complicated and indeed relied upon belt final drive when others – P&M, Royal Enfield etc – with military contracts had the newer, more

"HIS"
TRIUMPH

serving his country. OUR triumph producing TRIUMPHS to assist in the triumph of the Empire.

TRIUMPH CYCLE Co., Ltd.,
COVENTRY.

In answering this advertisement it is desirable to mention "The Motor Cycle."

Above: *Military 'paperboy' delivers newspapers at the back of the French line. The Triumph is fitted with a Gloria sidecar.*

fashionable chain final drive. But the very success of the Triumph was its basic nature. It was flexible, easy to use and fairly immune to the hamfistedness of its operator and the lack of maintenance available in the field. All in all, a perfect military machine.

Triumph had once again been cute, with the men behind the military Model H Schulte and his works manager Charles Hathaway. Hathaway had joined Triumph soon after the diversification

into motorcycle manufacture and Schulte and he were a formidable team. Between them they'd overseen Triumph's progression from a bicycle maker that clipped Belgian-built engines to cycle frames, to one of the world's largest motorcycle manufacturers.

So the duo were ideal candidates to come up with a military machine. Originally, the Model A – a 499cc model, with either free-engine (clutch) facility or a three-speed hub gear – was

Above: *Filling up 'somewhere' in the Near East, June 1915*

Right: *The First Armoured Motor Battery, commanded by Sir John Willoughby. Photographed before heading overseas*

BRITISH MOTORCYCLES : **TRIUMPH**

Above: *Lieuts. Cecil S Burney (left) and Harris, back in England, engaged in training motorcyclists for despatch work at the front*

Right: *Corporal FN Foster, 31/2 hp Triumph, after 14 months on active service*

supplied, but this was replaced by the specially developed Model H. Rated at 4hp, the Model H had a separate three-speed gearbox which was controlled by a long lever mounted directly. Drive was by belt which – as Schulte and Hathaway

Above: *A Triumph with Gloria munitions-carrier sidecar, April 1916*

Left: *Corporal D maple, also 3 1/2 hp Triumph, also after 14 months on active service*

no doubt made sure the military knew – was more flexible and less likely to break than a chain. Old fashioned it may have been but it was tried, tested and trusty technology – and it ensured the Trusty Triumph its place in military folklore.

Cheap and Cheerful: Vintage Period – 1918-1930

After WWI, the world had changed. Personal transport was demanded by the masses, Triumph was happy to oblige – but the after the peak came a late-1920s trough.

Thanks to the sterling service of the Model H during WWI, come peace time, then the Triumph brand was seen as an embodiment of all that was good with Britain. The Trusty Triumph had served its country with distinction and often without complaint, like so many young men. The people trusted the Triumph brand thanks in large part due to its war record.

Immediately after the war, the public was crying out for personal transport. So many men – and indeed women – who would never have left their villages, never have travelled abroad, never have driven or ridden a motor vehicle, now had. Though the war had inflicted terrible suffering it had also changed the perceptions and aspirations of a generation and indeed generations to come. There was a feeling that life was for living and enjoying and motorcycles and the freedom they offered were an important part of that.

Triumph's initial post-WWII range was based upon a version of old faithful, the Model H. But there was soon a big shake-up – Claude Holbrook, Bettmann's old friend, joined as general manager and then later in the year, Schulte, who had done so much, was

Above: Glasgow Team Trial, 1921, Mr Simons leaving the start

invited to resign, which he did with a £15,000 gratuity payment. Schulte and Bettmann had become increasingly far apart in their view of where the company was going and with Bettmann employing his old ally Holbrook, and the majority shareholding enjoyed by Bettmann, one imagines that Schulte's position had become untenable.

Bettmann – and surely Holbrook –

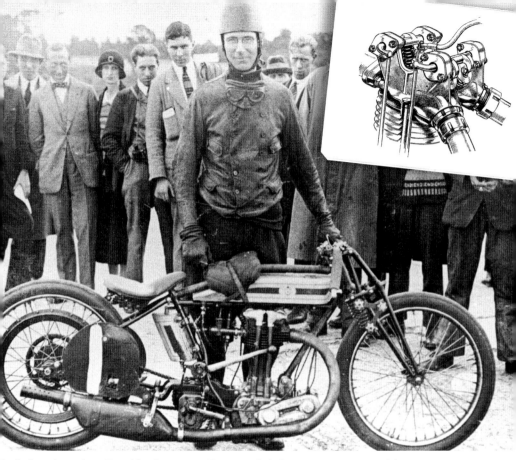

had the view that diversification was the future, while Schulte had been of the opinion it would be better to improve and continue to develop the core product, ie the motorcycles. But Bettmann's influence was more and it was he who had the final say and Schulte who had to leave. The Triumph Motor Company was established in 1922 and the first four-wheeler was a 1400cc

Above: *Victor Horsman, Brooklands special*
Far Above: *The four-valve Ricardo, 1921*

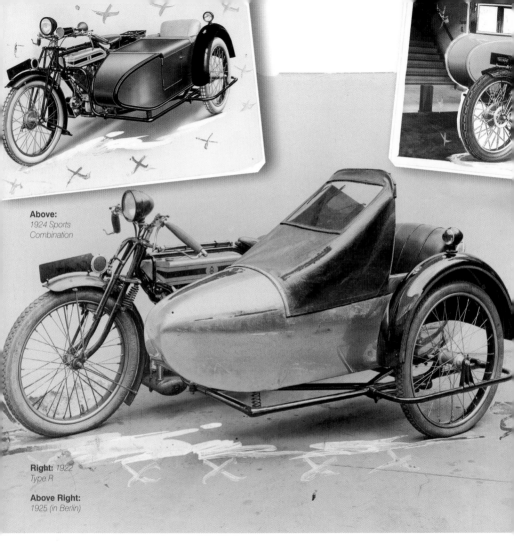

Above:
1924 Sports Combination

Right: *1922 Type R*

Above Right:
1925 (in Berlin)

light saloon, built at the abandoned Hillman car plant in Coventry.

The motorcycle range had been developed in so much as that all chain drive had been adopted as had Triumph's own three-speed gearbox on the new 4hp SD (Sprung Drive). The company had also introduced a sportster – the four-valve Ricardo, which was basically an overhead valve sporting

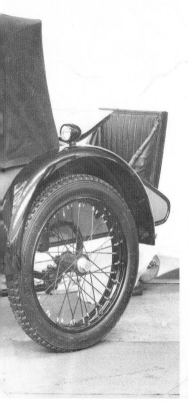

engine put into the standard rolling chassis. But the boom after WWI was nearly over and the world was heading for recession.

It was in this climate that Triumph

Above:
1928-model N De Luxe

Right & Far Right: *The 1923 346cc unit-construction model, with outside flywheel*

1925 MACHINES on the ROAD

The 494 c.c. TRIUMPH

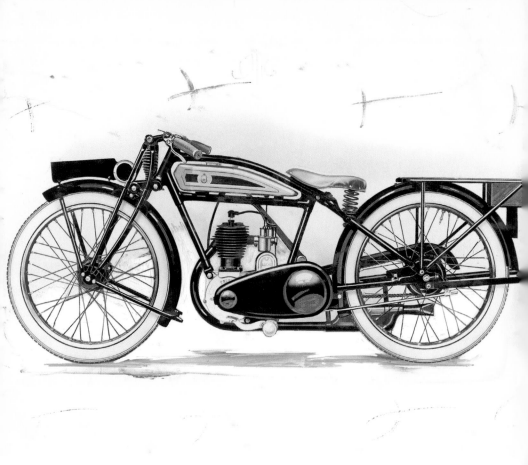

launched the Model P, a 500cc machine which sold for the hard-to-believe figure of £42-17s-6d. There were teething problems, but 20,000 were shifted fairly rapidly and with the problems solved for the MkII version, at times production was topping 1000 units a week. The company was flying

Left: Bob Pollard, Crewkerne, Somerset, on his Ricardo, 1923

ROBERT (Bob) POLLARD, CREWKERNE
1923-ISH
PHOTO- WILLIAM POLL[...]

Above: 1928 LSD

...nd by now, the works – based in Priory Street – covered an area of 500,000 square feet and employed 3000 people. It was a massive operation but as the decade progressed, Triumph was experiencing the reality that even the biggest companies are not immune to world recession.

Style and Substance: Post-Vintage – 1931-1939

Coming off the back of the 1920s, Triumph was still a massive operation, but cracks were beginning to appear and the motorcycle side of the business was starting to suffer. It seemed cars were now the priority and the two-wheelers were relegated to a supporting role. There was the odd new model but in reality everything had stagnated and not much was happening. That, though, was all going to change.

Valentine Page joined Triumph in 1932, from Ariel. His impact may not have been immediate – but it was to be decisive in the history of Triumph. It was the 1934 season before the first of the Page machines made their bow. Among them was a simple, inoffensive overhead valve 250cc machine, coded the L2/1. I may not have been groundbreaking, bu it was solid, well-built and surprisingly sprightly. What was more exciting wa the 6/1, a 650cc parallel twin that wa envisaged as primarily a sidecar tug In between the L2/1 and the 6/1 wa a whole new range, but it was thes two machines that were to set th groundwork for Triumph's renaissance.

The new range proved a success and Triumph was back on track, at least with its quality of product. However, all wa not well with the company's finances and a receiver had been appointed before in January 1936, Jack Sangster, agreec a relatively seamless takeover of the motorcycle side of the business, replacing

TRIUMPH

For Faultless Riding

MILLIER

Above: *E Kendrew, Scarborough Motor Club Freak Hillclimb, July 1938*

Above: *Miss Marie Vernon, secretary of Deansgate Mart Ltd, Manchester, starting for Liverpool after taking over the 150cc Triumph which was ridden round England by Triumph agents. Miss Marie Burke, the well-known actress, wishes her 'bon voyage'. The Motor Cycle, March 1935.*

Bettmann as company chairman. In the meantime, Page had departed – but next came perhaps the most significant appointment in Triumph's illustrious history, the recruitment of Edward Turner. Turner and Triumph were to become inextricably linked, their destinies woven together for all time.

Edward Turner was a bright young man, born in 1901. He had designed an

Above: *GS Gadfield with 14ft boat behind his trials combo, October 1935*

Left: *The 1933 Ilkley Grand National; R Thompson (493cc Triumph) at Dob Park Splash*

Right: *1931
350cc WL; price
£37-17s-6d*

Right: *1933
250cc WA*

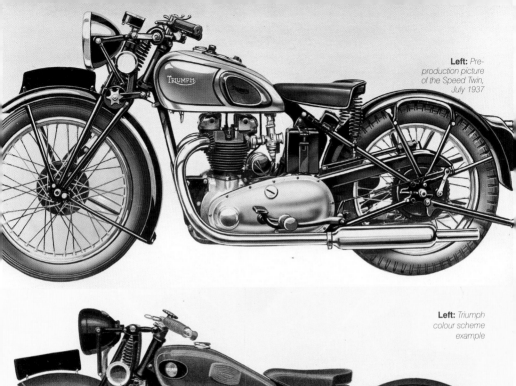

Left: *Pre-production picture of the Speed Twin, July 1937*

Left: *Triumph colour scheme example*

1935
Model 6/1

Above: *Freddie Clarke, March 1937, Triumph stock machine test*

overhead camshaft single and the famous Square Four, which of course put into production by Ariel. It was Ariel that also benefited from Turner's seemingly Midas touch when he introduced the Red Hunter range of 250, 350 and 500cc singles, with a bit of glitz and a catchy name about them. On his arrival at Triumph, Turner replicated his work at Ariel and Triumph's solid singles were given a going over. What emerged was the Tiger 70, 80 and 90 line-up – handsome black, silver and chrome singles aimed squarely at the man who would have

bought a Red Hunter the year before.

But more was to come – and what news it was. Probably the most important single step ever taken by Triumph was the decision to launch Edward Turner's Speed Twin on the public in 1938. It was a revelation, a sensation and set the template for the rest of Triumph's history. Finished in amaranth red and chrome, the Speed Twin was joined by the high performance Tiger 100 in 1939 and Triumph had now moved smoothly back into position as one of Britain's leading motorcycle making companies.

Above: *12 October 1933; 500 miles in 500 minutes, Brooklands, Surrey*

Far Above: *1936 Model 5/10; price £80*

Above: *1938 Tiger 70*

Right: *1939 500cc 5S*

Far Right: *Allan Jefferies, International Six Days Trial selection tests, July 1939*

Far Bottom: *1935 150cc XO5/5*

WWII: War Service & War Damage – 1939-194

At the outbreak of WWII, Triumph was riding the crest of a wave. The single cylinder Tigers were among the best and most attractive of their type on offer, while the Speed Twin and Tiger 100 had raised the bar in terms of sporting solos. Things could not be going better for the Coventry-based concern. So, war came at a particularly bad time for the personal interest of the company.

However, between 1938 and 1941, around 10,000 side-valve 3SWs were supplied to the military, replacing the 3S. In 1940, around 1500 5SWs were also supplied. WWII did have a huge, direct impact on Triumph when, in November 1940, the factory was heavily bombed. As well as destroying a lot of machines – a number of 3SWs plus the first batch of 50 of the 3TW model, a 350cc twin which Triumph had planned to produce in large numbers – much tooling, plans and spares were destroyed too, particularly for the 3TW. Mercifully – and incredibly – there was no loss of life in the Triumph works. But the raids left Triumph homeless.

The bombing assault in which Triumph's works were destroyed was of an unprecedented level. On the evening of 14 November 1940, over 500 Luftwaffe bombers launched an attack on Coventry on a scale never before seen. The assault lasted over 10 hours and left much of the city devastated, with wave after wave of aircraft dropping bombs indiscriminately, destroying many buildings, including the

MERIDEN 1943.

BRITISH MOTORCYCLES : **TRIUMPH**

Right: *The despatch riders of the women's Royal Naval Service. 1941*

city's 14th century cathedral.

Bombing began at 7.20pm and it wasn't until 6.15am that the all-clear was sounded. The raids on Coventry were termed 'legitimate' by the German high command, based on the fact that the city was home to so much heavy industry, making everything from bombs, to

aeroplanes, to of course motorcycles, for the war effort. In fact, the RAF had bombed Munich – home to the Nazi party – on 8 November so many read the Coventry raid as a revenge attack.

As the relentless 14 November attack on Coventry continued, so the resistance weakened. By 2am defences

YOU!

ARE YOUR TYRE
PRESSURES O.K.?

HOW ABOUT
YOUR SPARE?

ANY CUTS?

were ravaged, with anti-aircraft defences running out of ammunition. Still they came though and it wasn't until 5am that there was any sign of let up. By the time it was all over, 554 people had been killed, 4330 homes destroyed and three quarters of the city's factories destroyed. It wasn't all Coventry had to endure though, as in April 1941 the city was again targeted, this time with raids of between six and eight hours.

After the November mauling, Triumph moved into an old foundry building at Warwick and set-to producing the 3HW model, based on the Tiger 80, while Triumph set about selecting a new site for the factory to be rebuilt on. A location at Meriden was secured and work commenced in July 1941, with some machinery in situ by March the next year and it was fully operational soon after. Triumph had a new home.

Right: *Bren gun carrier, 1940*

Establishing the Brand Post WWII – 1945-50

Come the end of WWII and it was a case of getting back to business. After six years of hard, brutal war, peace came about – but it wasn't now a case of 'an easy time for all'. There were still massive shortages and Britain, as a country, was in huge debt.

For 1946 Triumph had a range up and ready to go, which of course drew heavily on the pre-WWII models, the Tiger 100 and Speed Twin, but also featured a new 350cc twin – the 3T – plus a 350cc single, the 3H, which was basically a civilianised version of the 3HW. All the new models, though, differed in one important way from the pre-war examples in that all were fitted with telescopic forks.

Edward Turner, always confident that Britain would emerge from the hostilities victorious, had begun to think of how best to develop 'his' motorcycle manufacturer relatively early on during WWII. To that end, he'd decided that he needed to gain a strong presence in America and had been working on doing so during the war and as early as 1946, was exporting Triumphs across the Atlantic.

Another important happening for Triumph during the period was in 1946, when Irishman Ernie Lyons won the Senior Manx GP on a Triumph twin. The machine, based upon a Tiger 100 but fitted with an all-alloy top end as used on wartime generator

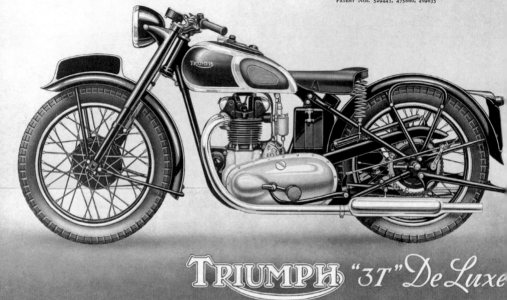

TRIUMPH "3T" De Luxe

Above: *Triumph 3T De Luxe*

units, was developed in the works by Freddie Clarke, who had campaigned Triumphs pre-WWII and indeed held – and still holds – the 350cc and 750cc class lap records at Brooklands, set on a 350cc Triumph single and overbored 503cc Speed Twin. The legality of Lyons' machine was, in truth, somewhat dubious – the Manx was supposedly an 'amateur' event for privately owned machines and this one had been developed at the works and even sported a prototype sprung hub rear suspension set-up. Lyons, riding for the most part in driving rain, won at 76.74mph. A replica went on sale in 1947 and Don Crossley used a Grand Prix to win the 1948 Senior Manx GP.

Left: *HRH Prince Bertil on the first Thunderbird in Sweden, 13 December 1949*

Centre: *Triumph brochure, 1947*

Right: *The Speed Twin, 1949*

Far Top: *The still-born Tiger 85, 1946*

Far Bottom: *Tiger 100s used by customs officials in the Russian zone of Austria, 1948*

Triumph

Above: *1947 Tiger 100*

Far Above: *Ernie Lyons winning the 1946 Manx Grand Prix*

In 1949, Edward Turner introduced two of his most famous developments – the headlamp nacelle and the Triumph Thunderbird. The nacelle went a long way to tidying up the handlebar area, introducing a flowing element and neatening what had always been a 'scruffy' area on a motorcycle. Coupled with Triumph's neat, slim telescopic forks, it moved the machines into a whole new era from the 'cobbled together' look of pre-WWII girder forks/exposed springs/separate speedometer, into an altogether neater arrangement – which surely pleased Turner greatly.

The Thunderbird was a by-product of Turner's success in pushing Triumph in America. The brand had established a strong reputation Stateside, mainly on

Below: *Grand Prix, 1949*

the back of the Tiger 100, but the cry had gone up for 'more cubes'. For a nation raised on a diet of big capacity V-twins, cubic capacity was all important and so though they loved the Tiger 100 and it outperformed the big sloggers they were used to (a good litl'un will beat a bad big 'un), the adapted adage 'a good litl'un, will always get beaten by a good big 'un' meant the Americans wanted a good big 'un as well. And they got one, with the 'T-bird'.

On Top of the World
Boom Years – 1951-1960

Triumph entered the 1950s in a position of power. In Edward Turner the company possessed the man most would like running their company, a man seemingly with the happy ability to turn to gold everything he touched. One of the products that was the result of Turner's said Midas touch was the 649cc Thunderbird, which at the beginning of the 1950s, was arguably the most desirable of motorcycles out there, certainly for the man in the street. And the T-Bird was backed up by a range that was packed full of quality, from the friendly 350cc 3T, to the sporting Tiger 100, the trusty Speed Twin and the competition-biased Trophy and Grand Prix. Life was, indeed, good at Meriden.

And it carried on in a similar vein through the early 50s. Though some mumbled that Turner's sprung hub wasn't up to much, it didn't stop Triumphs selling well indeed. But Turner was aware that his company didn't have an entry level machine, one to tempt the youngsters and 'hook' them onto the Triumph, so that they'd be buyers for life. It was something he attempted to address with the Terrier, a 150cc single which had styling aping the bigger models in the range. It was launched in November 1952 and it and its developments were to spawn quite a dynasty themselves.

Soon after the Terrier barked into the sunlight, in 1954 the Tiger 110 roared into being. Those insatiable, capacity-

ON TOP OF THE WORLD

Right: *When Mr and Mrs WK Nelson of Hollywood arrived at Triumph to take delivery of a Thunderbird and Swallow Jet 80 sidecar outfit, they had no previous experience of motorcycling. After driving instructions on the work's sportsfield, the couple left for a three-months' continental trip. The Motor Cycle, June 1952*

Below: *1952 ISDT machine*

Far Right: *Whittaker's Cub-based racer, Mallory March 1958*

Far Bottom: *The Geneva show, 1958*

NLF 263

Above: *Triumph rider with pillion, 1955*

hungry Americans had been briefly sated by the Thunderbird but now they wanted more! So, Turner responded with the Tiger 110 (Ton-ten) which was based upon the T-Bird, but boasted bigger valves and ports, higher compression pistons, different camshafts – and an all-new swinging arm frame.

In 1953 a small-budget film, The Wild One, loosely based around the

Above: *Six Americans at Stratford-on-Avon in July 1952, on their Thunderbirds*

Left: *Crowded Brixham harbour, November 1955*

Top: *Tiger 100, 1953*

Centre: *John Giles, winner Bramley scramble, April 1957*

happenings at Hollister in 1947, was made. The central character of the film was disaffected youth 'Johnny' played by Marlon Brando. The Wild One – which shocked audiences in its day – placed Johnny on a Thunderbird and despite legend saying Triumph apparently

BRITISH MOTORCYCLES : **TRIUMPH**

tried to distance themselves from the movie, an iconic image was established and Triumph's name boosted. It was probably no coincidence that another icon of 'disaffected youth', James Dean, had a Triumph in 'real life'.

The swinging arm frames spread

Above: *Either ends of the range – Bonnevilles and Cubs for export, 1959 models*

Right: *The 1958 range on display in Daytona*

"They stood back and once again admitted that for sheer functional beauty, the Triumph is unbeatable from stem to stern"

TRIUMPH
THE WORLD'S BEST AND
EAST... MOTORCYC...

Above: *Jack Dale, clad in bathing trunks, on Bus Schaller's Thunderbird, Bonneville, 1954*

through the range and then on 6 September 1956, there was an important happening at Bonnneville Salt Flats, when Johnny Allen achieved a speed of 214mph with his fully streamlined, tuned Triumph twin. It was to prove an important event in the history of Triumph.

Another big event was the launch of the first unit-construction (engine and gearbox in unit) twin, a cute 350 named

the 3TA Twenty-One. It was a big step and arguably the most significant event since launch in the history of Triumph twins – the progressing from a separate engine and gearbox to all unit set up. This was to be followed by a 'unit' Speed Twin a year later, though the 'big bikes' (the 650s) saw out the 50s as pre-units.

But, in retrospect, probably the biggest event of the period for Triumph

BRITISH MOTORCYCLES : **TRIUMPH**

was the first appearance in its line-up of a model with a name that will forever by synonymous with – the Bonneville (thanks for the name, Johnny A!). Launched for the 1959 season, the twin-carb sportster – again aimed squarely at those power mad Americans – would go on to be well known...

Kings of Cool: 1961-1970

Far Right: *Tiger 100 on test, August 1966*

Far Top: *Thruxton 500 mile winners 1961, John Holder (seated) and Tony Godfrey. T120 Bonneville*

Come the 60s and for Triumph and the UK, times were good. Motorcycle sales had reached an all-time peak in the UK in 1959 and Turner's Triumph had a fair slice of the pie and was still doing very nicely, thank you, into the 1960s. The Bonneville was the bike that all the little boys (and rockers) wanted. The other 650cc twins still offered fabulous value-for-money, while the half-litre version, if anything, was a better buy still. The decade started with Triumph relying upon the 'pre-unit' construction engine and gearbox for its 650cc machines but then for the 1963 season, the company switched to the unit construction format, used so successfully on the 350 and 500cc models. The 'unit'

idea neatened up the whole engine assembly and was to form the basis of all models that were to emerge from the old Triumph factory – it was arguably the last major development ever to come from Meriden. One of the biggest happenings of the decade for Triumph though was the announcement, in December 1963, that Edward Turner was retiring, from 1 January 1964.

Though the Turner–devised 'bathtub' styling used in the early 60s wasn't universally loved, it wasn't universally loathed either – and it was a far more successful effort at fashionable enclosure than many of the other manufacturers had managed. But what Triumph had always done best was big,

Above: *The likely lads, 1963*

Above Right: *Speed Twin being used by Fijian police, 1966*

high-speed, hairy-chested twins – and that was something that dawned on the company as the decade wore on.

So, as time went by, Triumph focused its intentions on the 'Bonneville end' of the market. First sign was the introduction of the T100SS, which looked like its bigger Bonneville brother apart from colouring, while the 1963 Tiger 90 was basically a baby Bonnie. Though the 350cc twin was of single carb – and had bikini fairings – it was

THE 200 MILE AMA CLASSIC
DAYTONA

79

which
victory
National
Race at

s toughest
the com-
nore set a
record of
t two m.p.h.
ous record
hine basically
) in your local

*Left: A selection
of Triumph
promotional
material*

MOUNTAIN CUB T 20/M

TRIUMPH

200 c.c. O.H.V. SINGLE CYLINDER.
A truly fine lightweight trail bike. The Mountain Cub will take you up hills, over dusty trails, into the back
A favorite for hunters and fishermen because it gets them where it's tough to go. It can crawl at a snail
yet accelerate to 60 m.p.h. and turn on a dime. There's a 4-speed, special wide ratio gearbox for trac
performance in rough going and a regular fourth gear for highway cruising without troublesome chain re s
changing. The Cub is the only fully equipped, standard trail bike with no extras to buy. All good reasons to buy

FOR SPECIFICATIONS AND TECHNICAL DATA S⁻⁻ **PAGES 10 AND 11**

MOTOR CYCLE

UMPH

t Motorcycle
World
V 8 D

Above: *Malcolm Uphill, winner 1969 Production TT, at an average speed of 99.99mph*

finished in the Bonnie's Alaskan white colour. The imitation increased, too, with the Tiger 90's bikini dropped and it became, pure and simply, a 'baby Bonnie.' Gradually, all 'enclosure' disappeared from the Triumph range and then in 1967 both the nacelle and the Thunderbird took their final bow too. It was apparent that the market,

for Triumph, was for big and beefy machines.

American sales were still strong, backed up by success in competition, but in the smaller capacities, Triumph were lagging behind and the threat from the Orient from gathering pace. While they may have been nice people on all those Hondas, they were still forming

brand loyalty to the – relative – upstart company from Tokyo, especially in the US. Though Triumph toyed with a 350cc twin, it never made it into series production – though the 750cc Trident did. It was just a shame those pesky people from Honda released a overhead camshaft electric start four at around the same time…

Triumph, though, had another starring role in the 60s when Steve McQueen – an unashamed Triumph fan, who'd ridden Triumphs in the ISDT – used a thinly disguised Triumph to complete a Great Escape, while Bob Dylan wore his brand loyalty on his chest for his Highway 61 Revisited album cover – though the great rocker had a big crash on his Bonnie in 1966, seriously beating himself up.

On the race tracks, Triumph started the 60s as a non-participant, but gradually as the decade passed, came into things, especially as production racing took hold. The culmination was Malcolm Uphill's famous 99.99mph race average (and 100mph lap) in the 750cc class of the Production TT in 1969, which followed on from John Hartle's win in the inaugural 1967 event.

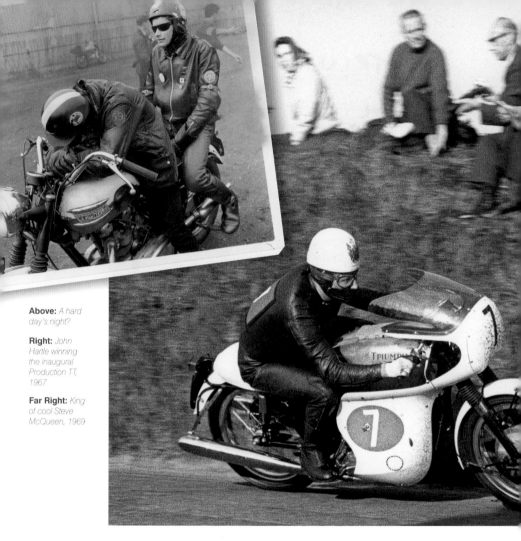

Above: *A hard day's night?*

Right: *John Hartle winning the inaugural Production TT, 1967*

Far Right: *King of cool Steve McQueen, 1969*

Far Right: *Ken Heanes, 1961 ISDT*

Far Top: *Percy Tait on the works 500, at Ramsey Hairpin, 1968 Senior TT*

650 c.c. TRIUMPH THUNDERBIRD (6T)

Elsewhere on the racetracks, Percy Tait – for so long a Triumph tester – stunned the GP world with his performances on a tuned 500cc twin, the highlight of which was a stunning second place in the 1969 Belgian GP.

Though the threat from the east did perhaps look somewhat ominous, there was still reason aplenty for optimism at Meriden.

The Slippery Slope: 1971–1980

Triumph started the 70s in a somewhat precarious position. Though the 'big bikes' were selling well, that was a good job, because there wasn't – apart from a couple of rebadged BSA singles – much else in the line-up. The 750cc Trident was a machine which boasted the performance to trouble the Japanese – and now Italian – emerging 'superbike' machines, while the 650cc range was still proving popular too. However, that was pretty much it while the Japanese factories, with Honda being joined by Yamaha, Suzuki and Kawasaki, were showing no signs of relenting in their plans for range expansion.

Triumph had been toying with its 350cc Bandit, but that proved stillborn, while the 1972 oil-in-frame redesign also proved unpopular. Dark clouds were gathering, while a new generation of motorcyclists, brought up on Japanese machines, had higher expectations in terms of what they demanded from a brand new motorcycle – and with Japanese options appearing with regularity in the big capacity classes, those expectations could now be met. Add to that the fact that the Italian industry had now discovered a taste for making 'big bikes,' with the likes of Ducati, Moto Guzzi, Laverda and Benelli coming to the party, and tough times were undoubtedly just around the corner.

19   19A

Above: *Bonnie bend swinging, 1979*

Above Right: *The UK spec Jubilee Bonnie.*

Right: *Arthur Browning causes a splash during the 1971 ISDT*

Far Right: *Jubilee certificate*

RIDE A LIVING LEGEND

Certificate of Ownership

This is to certify that

is the Owner of a Triumph Silver 750,
one of a thousand special versions of the Triumph
Bonneville 750 motorcycle manufactured as a
Limited Edition by Meriden Motorcycles Limited
for sale in the United Kingdom, in honour of
the Silver Jubilee of the reign of Her Majesty
Queen Elizabeth II

SPECIMEN
ONLY

Chairman,
Meriden Motorcycles Limited

Authorised Triumph Dealer

Date

Silver 750 Limited Edition

Above Right: The still-born Bandit Street Scrambler – it was officially dropped from the range in August 1971 though none were ever sold

However, in the early 70s, there was a bright cloud offered in the performance of Triumph – and sister BSA – machines, including the remarkable production racing triple, Slippery Sam. Every year between 1971 and 1975, the redoubtable 'Sam' clinched victory in the 750cc class of the Production TT, and his run of success was only ended by a ruling which outlawed bikes over five years old from the 'Proddie' TT.

It was also in the early 70s that one of

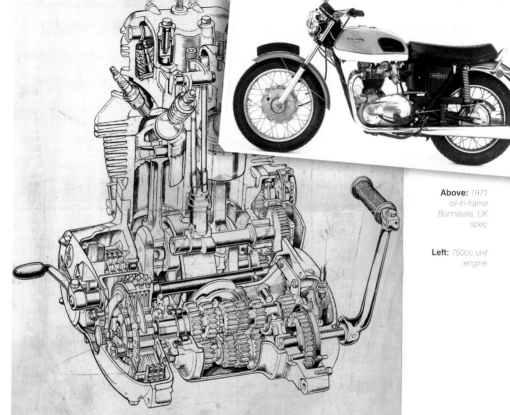

Above: *1971 oil-in-frame Bonneville, UK spec*

Left: *750cc unit engine*

the now most highly prized – and priced – 'collectable' Triumphs emerged, the Craig Vetter-styled X75 Hurricane. Now tagged 'the world's first factory custom' the striking Triumph came about because of US resistance to the original styling of the Trident/Rocket 3 range. Vetter's design – actually conceived in 1969 – has become a cult classic, but at the time the model's high

Above: *Rob North-framed Trident racer*

Right: *Ride like the law, 1972*

Name of Job ~~MOTORCYCLE~~

Ad No.   Date   26/2

Studio No. 008770

Mono ✓   2 Colour

Screen 100   Size % 220%

Right Reading Negs KH   Wrong Reading Pos

Wrong Reading Negs   Right Reading Pos

Sent to   Date

Left: *Dave Croxford – partnered by Alex George – won the 1975 Production TT on 'Slippery Sam', the famous racing Trident. 'Sam' was a TT winner five times in a row, this year the last*

Below: *1975 750cc Triumph Trident*

price and scarcity meant they were a rare sight.

As the 70s progressed, so did Triumph's troubles. Though the oil-in-frame twin was revised to general satisfaction and a T160 version of the Trident introduced, there were no new models, just 'developments.' Added to that was a series of union-led strikes and general unrest, plus the ever-strengthening Japanese – and to a lesser extent, Italian – makers introducing newer and ever more complex models. By the end of the 70s, the writing was writ large on the wall. And what it said wasn't pleasant.

Death and Rebirth: 1981–1990

Far Right: *1982 Bonneville Royal, at Meriden*

As the 80s dawned Triumph was, to put it bluntly, on its knees. Though there had been various attempts at new models – like the eight-valve TSS and the 'factory customs' (which, incidentally, though started by Triumph with the Hurricane had been wholly embraced by the Japanese) – there was nothing really 'new'. By the start of 1983, manufacture at Meriden had altogether ground to a halt and the end looked nigh for a company which just 15 or so years earlier had, in the Bonneville, been building arguably the most well-known, desirable motorcycle in the world. Just a decade and a half earlier, Triumphs had been beloved of rock stars, movie icons and the motorcycling public – now,

as the 80s began, the company and its products appeared a relic of an era of which no one was interested in. It was, indeed, a rapid fall from grace.

With Triumph now broke and out of business, it was in late 1983 that a new name entered the rich history of Triumph. John Bloor, building magnate and entrepreneur, bought the name, all existing projects, the logos, the trademarks and everything else associated with the company. It may have seemed a strange decision to those looking on as Bloor had no history in motorcycling, or indeed even engineering, but he had proved himself a shrewd and successful businessman.

Meanwhile, the Triumph name

Below: *From 1982, the T140ES has more than a hint of BMW's successful R90/100S about it...*

Far Right: *TS8-1, an attempt at updating*

Above: The bright new hope, the TSS

Far Top: Early 80s Tiger trail was the last in a long line of off-road ohv twins

Far Bottom: The reintroduced Thunderbird name – a single carb 750

didn't completely disappear as John Bloor licensed out the rights to build twins to Les Harris, who continued to make a small, but steady, stream of Bonnevilles, while Bloor set about resurrecting the Triumph concern proper. A factory – built by Bloor's own company, naturally – was constructed on a 10-acre greenfield site on the outskirts of Hinckley. In the early days, though, there were no great proclamations about when, what or where Triumph was going to concentrate its efforts. Indeed, the building of the factory had been completed in a quiet, unobtrusive manner and it was 1988 when the motorcycle world really noticed that

Bloor had completed his factory. Still, the project was swathed in secrecy and no one was prepared to spill Bloor's secrets.

The first clue that things were happening was when in 1988, at a convention in the US, some castings were displayed but that was it. With the British motorcycling press itching

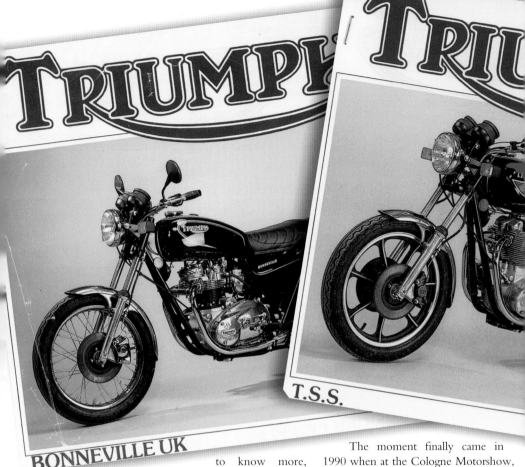

T.S.S.

BONNEVILLE UK

Above: *1983 Bonneville UK – as built by Les Harris under licence from 1985-88*

to know more, still mystery and secrecy shrouded the whole enterprise – the message was clear; we'll tell you when we're good and ready.

The moment finally came in 1990 when at the Cologne Motorshow, in Germany, the range of three and four-cylinder machines was shown and again at the Milan, Italy, show. Though the models were clearly influenced by Japanese

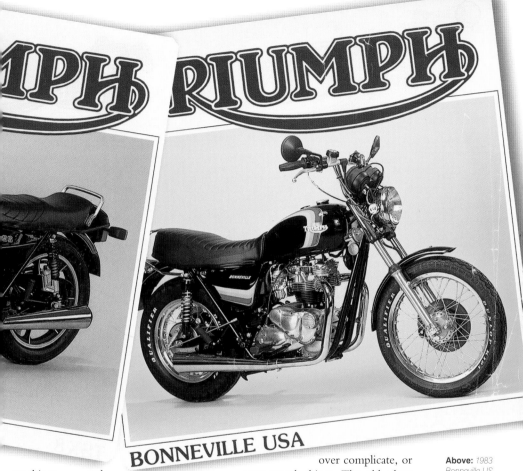

BONNEVILLE USA

machines – and some aimed barbed comments – the simple reality was Triumph had looked at what was being made and decided to not over complicate, or over stretch things. The old adage of not running before one can walk, seemed to hold true – and very sensible it seemed too.

Above: *TSS on the move*

Right: *Early 750cc prototype Trident, as unveiled to the world's press in autumn 1990*

Far Right: *The shape of things to come – the Phoenix 900, May 1983*

BRITISH MOTORCYCLES : **TRIUMPH**

Getting Established: 1991-2000

Far Right: *The lights shining brightly at the thriving Triumph factory*

In 1991 the first brand new motorcycles bearing the Triumph name appeared in dealer showrooms, for the first time in years. By April, some models were on sale and for September the full range was available. Canny businessman that he his, Bloor had realised that he needed to have the trust and support of the retail industry if his venture even had a chance of succeeding. To that end, a whole dealer network had been set up – and assured that the product they were going to get to sell would be well-made and the dealer wouldn't find itself correcting basic problems which were the fault of the factory; sadly, something that had been a major problem at the end of the Meriden days. The fact that Bloor was prepared to go to these lengths meant that the dealers had faith in him and his product – a great basis on which to start a working relationship.

The initial 'relaunch' models didn't attempt to be anything particularly revolutionary or even evocative of what had gone before – it was just a case of establishing a foothold in the market. To that end Triumph went for a modular concept, with a six-model launch range which consisted of the Trident 750 and 900, Daytona 750 and 1000 and Trophy 900 and 1200. The 750 and 900cc models were all triples, with the 1000 and 1200 versions four cylinder. However, all models shared

Number one machine shop
Components stores
Quality control area
Number two machine shop
Tube preparation
Welding shop
Casting pre-treatment
Paint pre-treatment
Painting shop
Assembly tracks
Final inspection
Packing and dispatch
Reception and main offices

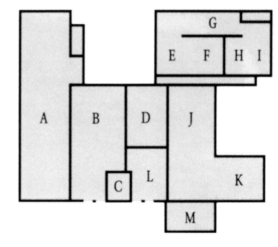

the same chassis, fuel tanks, engine components (and cylinder bore) and running gear while subtle differences in wheelbase were attributed to different length forks and suspension variations. It had been decided that it was crucial to Triumph establishing an identity that there was a three in the range – again,

reasoning which proved sound as it is unquestionably for its triples which Triumph is best known today.

The early models quickly proved popular and gained a reputation for being 'overbuilt' – Bloor and his team didn't want to upset those dealers to who they'd promised that the new models would be of a high quality

and to that end Triumph had over-engineered in the interest of strength and reliability, shrewdly reasoning it would be a good reputation to establish.

It soon became apparent that triples would be the future and more three cylinder models appeared, with the off-road Trophy and 'semi-sports' Sprint – a halfway house between the Trident and the Trophy. But, cried many, where were machines to appeal to the 'traditionalist' – and where were the most famous names from the Triumph portfolio?

The first answer came with the Thunderbird, launched for 1995, then joined soon after by the similarly

Above: *Trophy 1200, 1992*

Far Top: *1994 Tiger 900*

Far Bottom: *Speed Triple racer on the Triumph stand, 1994 Sporting Show*

Left: *1994 Daytona 900*

Above: *Race ace Phil Read, Mallory Park, Past Masters Race 1997*

Above: *Trophy 900 by the dock of the bay, 1991*

styled Adventurer. It marked a new, clear direction for Triumph, possibly moving away from where the restart had begun and into different territory. Also launched for 1995 was the 'naked' musclebike, the Speed Triple.

For 1997, came a new direction of sportsters, the T595 Daytona and the T509 Speed Triple, with redesigned Trophies, Sprints, Tigers and a new 600, the TT600, all added to the range.

Now that Triumph was back, it was a case of building a secure base in the marketplace.

Onwards and Upwards: 2000 – Present

Far Right: *2008 Sprint ST on the move.*

It had to happen – it was just a case of when. The moment had been speculated on ever since the first new Triumph had appeared and, for 2001, the famous Bonneville name was once more in the Triumph range. Aimed squarely at the retro market, the new Bonneville was however a fully modern motorcycle. Powered by a 790cc parallel twin, the Bonneville was not supposed to be the rip snorting sportster its original forebear had been but was instead an all round more friendly motorcycle, with looks that aped the original. Although some were disappointed, others immediately understood what the Bonneville was – an alternative to a certain motorcycle from Milwaukee that had done OK over the years, as well as a rival to the Japanese made retros and cruisers. And of course this one had Triumph written on the petrol tank.

The Bonneville has remained a mainstay of the Triumph range, with the firm realising that the base model could be developed to fill other niches, hence the launch of the Thruxton cafe racer version (2003) and the Scrambler (2005), while the more powerful, newer developed 865cc engine eventually found its way into the basic Bonneville. For 2008 there was a further advance for the Bonnevilles when they were switched to fuel injection.

However, the early 'noughties' wasn't all plain sailing as in 2002 the Hinckley

Above: *T100 Bonneville in the snow, Christmas 2005*

Centre: *Sprint RS, 2003*

plant was subject to a potentially devastating fire, and though production was massively disrupted Triumph was soon back, stronger than ever.

New models have continued to come apace. In the ultra-competitive 600cc supersports class, the initial TT600 was replaced by a more focused machine, the Daytona 600. The angular race-rep immediately found favour, while

Triumph made a return to racing with the model in 2003, with the Valmoto team. Though success didn't come immediately, Triumph did claim a first TT win since the days of Slippery Sam when Kiwi Bruce Anstey took the Junior 600cc race. In the British championship, Scotsman Jim Moodie and young Englishman Craig Jones thrilled race fans with Jonesy claiming a victory at

Above: *It had to come – the new Bonneville, out for the year 2001*

Far Top:
*Bonneville
America, 2002*

Far Middle:
*Sporting an eye-
catching paint job*

Far Bottom:
TT600, 2002

Left: *Bonneville
Scrambler,
unveiled for 2006*

Above: *2002 Daytona 955i*

Centre: *2008 Tiger*

Donington Park – the team's last race as Triumph withdrew at season's end.

There have been plenty of other groundbreaking new models through the noughties too, with the awesome Rocket III (2300cc, three cylinders, masses of torque) illustrating Triumph's

willingness to plough its own furrow. Another example of that individuality ethos has been the 675cc Daytona. This machine is another competitor in the supersport 600 category – but while the earlier Daytona 600 went along the same lines as the Japanese, this one is all

Triumph's own thinking. And it has proved an immense hit – on the roads, and on the racetracks too, with Aussies Garry McCoy and Mark Aitchison carrying the fight at World Supersports level, while, at the time of writing, another Aussie, Glen Richards, leads the prestigious and competitive British Supersport championship.

So, Triumph remains and becomes increasingly competitive on so many levels – continuing to live up to the name bestowed upon his business by Siegfried Bettmann all those years ago.

Above: *The new Thruxton Bonnie at the Ace Café, 2004*

ONWARDS AND UPWARDS

Far Top: *2006*
Daytona 675

Far Bottom: *2003*
Speedmaster

Below: *Awesome*
2300cc Rocket III